WORKBOOK

FOR

FERVENT:

A Woman's Battle Plan to Serious, Specific, and Strategic Prayer

A Practical Guide To Implementing Priscilla Shirer's Book

LOGOS-PEN PRESS

This Book Belongs To:

_____

_____

_____

From:

_____

_____

TABLE OF CONTENTS

How To Use This Workbook

Welcome to the companion Workbook for Fervent: A Woman's Battle Plan to Serious, Specific, and Strategic Prayer. By giving you a systematic framework to dig deeper into the important teachings, self-reflection, and self-evaluation, this workbook is intended to supplement the original book. By actively participating in this workbook, you will improve your comprehension of the principles presented in the book and obtain insightful knowledge about your personal development.

Here Is Guidance On How To Use This Workbook Efficiently

1. Become familiar with the summary: Read the original book's synopsis that is given at the start of this workbook to get started. This will jog your memory and guarantee that you have a firm grasp of the book's key concepts and topics.

2. Dive Into the Chapters: This workbook's chapters are matched up with chapters in the original book. Start by reading the main points of each chapter. These courses give a succinct synthesis of the most important ideas covered and emphasize the most significant takeaways. Consider how these lessons relate to your own experiences and goals as you take your time learning and reflecting on them.

3. Practice Self-Reflection: For each chapter, there are several self-reflection questions that you may answer after reading the important teachings. These inquiries are meant to sharpen your comprehension and promote reflection. Spend some time attentively considering each question before jotting down your answers. Since this is a chance for personal development and self-discovery, be open-minded and truthful with yourself.

4. Make Your Journey Your Own: Keep in mind that this workbook is a tool for your growth. As you interact with the information, feel free to scribble down any new ideas, revelations, or instances that occur to you. Use the area given to record any individual comments, tales, or action plans that come to mind while you travel to personalize your experience.

5. Self-Evaluation: After this workbook, there is a section devoted to this activity called "Self-Evaluation." You may evaluate your development, establish goals for the future, and examine your progress in this area. Examine your revelations, viewpoint shifts, and the effect the book has had on your life honestly. Set objectives, develop concrete actions, and commit to continuing your personal development beyond the pages of this workbook in this part.

Keep in mind that this workbook is a helpful tool that promotes participation and introspection. It is a companion that will help you comprehend the original book more deeply and apply its lessons to your own life. Be patient with yourself, keep an open mind, and embrace the transforming potential of self-reflection and self-discovery as you embark on this adventure.

With the help of this workbook, enjoy your path of development and personal change.

LOGOS-PEN PRESS

Overview

The enthralling and enlightening book "Fervent: A Woman's Battle Plan to Serious, Specific, and Strategic Prayer" by Priscilla Shirer welcomes women on a deep journey of prayer and provides potent techniques to interact with God in a meaningful and deliberate manner. Shirer leads readers through the practice of passionate prayer in an emotive and powerful style, giving them the tools they need to overcome challenges, enjoy victories, and lead fulfilling lives.

Shirer understands the crucial role that prayer plays in women's lives in a society full of difficulties, pressures, and spiritual warfare. She reveals the extraordinary power of prayer to influence situations, relationships, and personal development, drawing on her own experiences and profound biblical understanding. Shirer talks directly to the hearts of the readers, inspiring a passion for prayer and a desire to strengthen their relationship with God via poignant tales, personal experiences, and biblical insights.

The book begins with an open examination of the struggles that women encounter daily, whether in their private life, interpersonal connections, sense of identity, or spiritual path. Shirer skillfully crafts her sentences, drawing the reader in and eliciting feelings of empathy and resonance. She places a strong emphasis on the need and value of prayer as a tool to combat the devil's plans and achieve triumph in all spheres of life.

Shirer urges readers to be serious, focused, and strategic as she lays out a prayer battle strategy for them. She encourages women to approach God with trust, bravery, and tenacity through ardent prayer. She offers helpful advice throughout the book on how to identify and attack weak spots like doubt, anxiety, resentment, and insecurity. Shirer gives readers the resources they need to create a customized prayer plan that is suited to their particular struggles and situations.

The author examines the effectiveness of prayer based on scripture and demonstrates how God's Word may be a source of fortitude, direction, and change. To help women match their hearts and minds with God's truth and promises, she provides straightforward instructions for adding scripture into prayer.

Shirer goes into the relevance of strategic prayer, highlighting the need of identifying and concentrating on certain spiritual assault points. She provides techniques to get over hurdles and experience breakthroughs as she walks readers through the process of locating and destroying the enemy's strongholds. Shirer displays the power of intentional prayer in bringing about long-lasting transformation and spiritual development via moving examples and personal experiences.

"Fervent" is a strong and compelling work that captivates the mind and rouses the spirit. Readers have a strong connection to Priscilla Shirer's writing because it is passionate and expressive. This connection inspires readers to keep going, recognize their spiritual power, and pray fervently and in a transformational way. She kindles a fire within readers with each page, challenging them to harness the tremendous power of prayer and to fully appreciate God's love, grace, and provision.

Any woman who wants to improve her prayer life, overcome challenges, and lead a life of meaning and success should read this book. It acts as a rallying cry for women, motivating them to begin a path of intense prayer that will bring about spiritual breakthroughs, heavenly favor, and a closer relationship with their Heavenly Father.

Strategy 1: Your Passion : Getting It Back When It's Gone

Key Lessons

1. Rediscovering your passion: Shirer stresses the value of rediscovering your passion once it has faded. She advises ladies to rekindle their excitement for the things that formerly made them happy by identifying those things. Women may seek God's direction and petition Him in prayer to reignite their passion, remind them of their mission, and enkindle a fire inside them.

2. Recognizing the enemy's strategies: The chapter examines how the adversary deliberately sabotages our zeal and works to lessen our ardor. Shirer encourages readers to detect the cunning ways the adversary may sap our zeal and rob us of our pleasure. We may craft tailored prayers to combat and conquer the various strategies employed against us by recognizing them.

3. Creating a unique prayer plan: To defend against the assaults on our passion, Shirer emphasizes the need of creating a unique prayer plan. She exhorts readers to record their prayers and declarations, pointing them to

Scripture as a potent defense against the devil's falsehoods. Women may strengthen their passion and thwart the devil's efforts to sap it by creating a specific prayer plan that helps them concentrate their prayers with goal and purpose.

4. <u>Seeking God's truth and perspective:</u> The chapter highlights the need of aligning our ideas and emotions with God's truth. Shirer encourages readers to seek God's viewpoint on their interests and situations, letting His Word mold their ideas and views. Our thoughts may be renewed and we can acquire a new perspective that stokes our zeal by immersing ourselves in Scripture and reflecting on God's promises.

5. <u>Praying fervently and consistently:</u> Shirer emphasizes how powerful prayer can be in regaining and maintaining our enthusiasm. She exhorts women to continue in prayer and believe that God will respond rather than give up or get disheartened. We allow God to operate in our lives, rekindling our fire and aligning our hearts with His purpose, by regularly placing our desire before Him.

Self-Reflection Questions

When was the last time you were really enthused about anything, and how might you get that zeal back?

_____

_____

_____

What particular strategies have the devil used to stifle your delight and dwindle your enthusiasm? How can you identify and combat such strategies via prayer?

_____

_____

_____

_____

_____

_____

_____

_____

_____

_____

_____

_____

_____

Have you created a unique prayer plan to defend your passion against assault? How can your prayer approach be strengthened and improved so that you can direct your prayers with purpose and intention?

_____

_____

_____

_____

_____

_____

_____

_____

_____

_____

_____

_____

_____

_____

Are your interests and circumstances the subject of your search for God's truth and perspective? To refresh your mind and get a new perspective, how can you immerse yourself in the Bible and reflect on its promises?

_____

_____

_____

_____

_____

_____

_____

_____

_____

_____

_____

_____

_____

How tenacious are you in your praying practice?
Bring your interests before God regularly, believing
that He would act in your life and rekindle your zeal.
If not, what steps can you take to develop more
patience and faith in your prayer life?

Does your passion suffer from any ingrained ideas or cognitive patterns? How can you give those things to God, connect your heart with His plan, and let His truth sway your opinions and beliefs?

_____

_____

_____

_____

_____

_____

_____

_____

_____

_____

_____

_____

_____

Life-Transforming Exercises

1. Keep a journal of your passions: Reflect on times in your life when you were enthusiastic about something. Give a thorough account of those events that include the feelings and reasons that led to them. Recall those moments when your enthusiasm was fervent and alive in this notebook as a source of inspiration and encouragement.

2. Prayer Declaration Cards: Design unique prayer declaration cards that are all about rekindling your passion. Make explicit statements and prayers on paper that support your goals and purposes. Use these cards to concentrate your prayers by carrying them about and often speaking God's truth and promises over your cause.

3. Scripture Meditation: Choose relevant texts from the Bible that relate to your interests and goals. Set aside some time each day to reflect on these Scriptures and let God's Word saturate your mind and heart. Think about each verse's significance and application to your area of interest, and allow the biblical truth to rekindle your excitement and broaden your outlook.

4. Passion Accountability Partner: Locate a dependable friend or mentor who can act as your accountability partner in your passion. They can support and encourage you by hearing about your goals, challenges, and requests for prayer. As you pursue and maintain your passion, come together often to review your progress, pray with one another, and give accountability.

5. Prayer Walks: Take part in purposeful prayer walks where you mix exercise with prayer. Find a special place to walk or just go for a stroll in the park. As you walk, pray particularly for the revival of your passion. A stronger connection and a revitalized feeling of purpose and enthusiasm may be cultivated by moving your body while speaking with God.

Strategy 2: Your Focus: Fighting the Real Enemy

Key Lessons

1. Recognizing the Real Enemy: The first lesson is to understand that our struggles are not with physical foes but rather with spiritual powers of evil. We can better concentrate our prayers and plans on defeating the true foe by changing our attention from humans to the enemy operating covertly.

2. Dealing with Deception: The adversary often tries to mislead and twist the truth, sowing doubt and confusion in our thoughts. We may withstand the devil's falsehoods and stand firmly in the truth by immersing ourselves in God's Word and allowing it to direct our thoughts and senses.

3. Exposing the adversary's Strategies: The adversary uses several tactics to obstruct our advancement and undermine our faith. We may anticipate his maneuvers and proactively engage in spiritual warfare and prayer by understanding and identifying his strategies.

4. Praying with Power: As Christians, we have been given power through Christ to defeat the adversary.

Understanding and using our spiritual authority in prayer enables us to successfully fend off the enemy's assaults and achieve victory in our lives.

5. Focusing on God's Promises: It's important to change our attention from our issues and difficulties to God's promises and faithfulness. We may energize our prayers with confidence and look for God's involvement and deliverance in our conflicts by deliberately reflecting on His Word and being steadfast in His truth.

Self-Reflection Questions

How often do you actively remind yourself that your struggles are not with physical enemies but rather with spiritual ones? How may your prayers and behavior be affected by this change in perspective?

_____

_____

_____

_____

_____

_____

_____

_____

_____

_____

_____

_____

_____

_____

Where in your life have you encountered lies or distortions of the truth perpetrated by the enemy? How can you spend as much time as possible in God's Word to refute these lies?

_____

_____

_____

_____

_____

_____

_____

_____

_____

_____

_____

_____

_____

Consider some particular tactics the adversary has used to obstruct your development or undermine your faith. How can you proactively wage a spiritual battle and pray against these strategies?

How self-assured are you in using Christ's control over you spiritually? How can you improve your knowledge of and use of this authority in your everyday life and prayers?

_____

_____

_____

_____

_____

_____

_____

_____

_____

_____

_____

_____

Consider if your attention is more often focused on issues and difficulties or God's promises and faithfulness. How can you consciously direct your prayers and thoughts to place a greater emphasis on His promises?

_____

_____

_____

_____

_____

_____

_____

_____

_____

_____

_____

_____

If you continually fuelled your prayers with confidence, remaining steadfast in God's Word, and anticipating His involvement and deliverance in your struggles, how would your prayer life change? What actions can you do to develop this praying style based on faith?

_____

_____

_____

_____

_____

Life-Transforming Exercises

1. Truth journaling: Begin a truth notebook where you may record any falsehoods or misleading ideas the adversary attempts to implant in your head. Provide a biblical truth from God's Word that corresponds to each untruth. To better grasp God's promises and battle the deceit of the adversary, consistently reflect on these realities.

2. Scripture Memory: Select important verses that reaffirm God's promises, truths, and your identity in Christ. Memorize and reflect on these verses every day. These verses should be said aloud as a powerful affirmation of truth whenever you experience periods of uncertainty or spiritual conflict.

3. Prayer Walks: Go on focused prayer walks in the areas of your life that need healing or are under assault. As you walk, pray fervently and strategically, focusing on the strongholds of the adversary and announcing God's dominion and triumph there. Allow your physical activity to represent your spiritual growth as you declare victory in prayer.

4. Accountability in Prayer Partner: Locate a dependable buddy or guide who shares your goal to develop your

prayer life and wage spiritual battle. Set up a regular gathering or check-in where you may discuss your needs, successes, and challenges. Pray with one another, encouraging one another while you go about battling the actual enemy.

5. War Room Visualization: Designate a location in your house as a "war room" where you may visualize your spiritual conflicts. Display particular prayer requests, verses, and successes in a notebook, whiteboard, or bulletin board. Remind yourself of God's faithfulness and your spiritual authority as you spend time here often praying and planning.

Strategy 3: Your Identity: Remembering Who You Are

Key Lessons

1. Embrace Your True Identity: Strategy 3 emphasizes the importance of remembering and embracing one's identity as a beloved child of God. Priscilla Shirer encourages women to recognize their inherent worth and value in God's eyes and to find strength, confidence, and purpose in their prayer life and everyday living.

2. Combat the Enemy's Lies: This strategy also calls for vigilance against the lies and deceptions of the enemy. Shirer emphasizes the need to recognize and counter negative thoughts and beliefs that seek to undermine our true identity. Through prayer and meditating on God's Word, women can overcome the enemy's attacks and embrace the truth of who they are in Christ.

3. Forgive and Release Past Hurts: Strategy 3 delves into the power of forgiveness in reclaiming one's identity. Shirer highlights the significance of releasing the burdens of past hurts, resentments, and offenses. By forgiving others and even oneself, women can experience healing and restoration, leading to a deeper connection with their identity in Christ.

4. Guard Against Comparison and Insecurity: Shirer addresses the common struggles of comparison and insecurity that women often face. She encourages women to focus on their unique calling and purpose, rather than being entangled in the trap of comparison. By guarding their hearts and minds against insecurities, women can step into their true identity and confidently fulfill the plans God has for them.

5. Walk in Authority and Purpose: The final lesson from this strategy is the call to walk in the authority and purpose that God has ordained for each woman. Shirer empowers women to recognize their spiritual authority in Christ and to step boldly into their God-given purpose. By walking in alignment with their true identity, women can become powerful agents of change and impact their spheres of influence for God's glory.

Self-Reflection Questions

Have you fully embraced your true identity as a beloved child of God, and how does this understanding impact your perspective on life and prayer?

_____

_____

_____

_____

_____

_____

_____

_____

_____

_____

_____

_____

Reflect on any recent negative thoughts or beliefs that may have undermined your sense of identity. How

can you counter these lies through prayer and meditating on God's Word?

Is there anyone in your life that you need to forgive or release from past hurts? How might embracing forgiveness lead to a deeper connection with your identity in Christ?

_____

_____

_____

_____

_____

_____

_____

_____

_____

_____

_____

_____

_____

In what areas of your life do you find yourself struggling with comparison and insecurity? How can you guard your heart against these traps and focus on your unique calling and purpose?

_____

_____

_____

_____

_____

_____

_____

_____

_____

_____

_____

_____

How do you perceive your spiritual authority in Christ, and how can you walk more confidently in that authority in your daily life?

_____

_____

_____

_____

_____

_____

_____

_____

_____

_____

_____

_____

_____

_____

Take a moment to reflect on the dreams, passions, and talents that God has placed within you. How can you step boldly into your God-given purpose and impact your spheres of influence for God's glory?

_____

_____

_____

Life-Transforming Exercises

1. Identity Affirmation Exercise: Take time each day to affirm your identity in Christ. Write down powerful affirmations that remind you of your worth, value, and purpose as a beloved child of God. Repeat these affirmations out loud, internalizing them and allowing them to shape your thoughts and beliefs about yourself.

2. Forgiveness Journaling Exercise: Set aside dedicated time to journal about any past hurts, resentments, or offenses that may be weighing you down. Write a letter to the person(s) involved, expressing your feelings and releasing any negative emotions. Then, choose to forgive them and release yourself from the burden of holding onto those hurts. Reflect on the freedom and peace that comes from forgiveness.

3. Scripture Reflection Exercise: Select specific Bible verses that speak to your identity, strength, and purpose in Christ. Write these verses on notecards and place them where you will see them regularly, such as your bathroom mirror, workspace, or car dashboard. Take moments throughout the day to reflect on these verses, allowing them to renew your mind and anchor you in God's truth.

4. Comparison Detox Exercise: For a week or longer, challenge yourself to take a break from comparing yourself to others. Whether it be on social media or in person, make a conscious effort to avoid comparing yourself to others. Instead, focus on your own individual journey, talents, and blessings. Appreciate the successes of others without allowing them to diminish your value or progress.

Strategy 4: Your Family: Fortifying the Lives of Those You Love

Key Lessons

1. Pray for individual needs: This tactic teaches us the importance of praying especially for each family member's needs. Recognize that every person is dealing with their struggles and difficulties. Spend some time learning about their particular problems and offer up fervent prayers for their safety, development, and well-being.

2. Be aware of enemy assaults and prepare for them: Recognize that the adversary aims to attack and sabotage family peace and togetherness. Determine the areas where the adversary is attacking your family in prayer while being attentive and strategic. Pray that nothing that seeks to sever the links of love and support within your family would cause division, dissension, or other problems.

3. Protect your family with God's Word: Make blessings, protection, and spiritual development declarations over your family members with the force of Scripture. Include

passages from the right context in your prayers, communicating God's promises and truth into their life. Ask God to help each member of your family to be firmly established in their status as God's children and to be led by His knowledge and mercy.

4. Pray for solid marriages and parent-child connections. Recognize the enormous impact that strong parent-child ties and successful marriages have on a family's overall well-being. Ask God to strengthen the ties of love, respect, and communication in your marriage and the marriages within your family by sincerely praying for them. Additionally, pray for the parent-child ties, requesting God's wisdom and direction for developing strong bonds and creating a supportive and caring atmosphere.

5. Promote a culture of prayer and faith: Create a culture where prayer and faith are important in your family. Set an example by engaging in regular and ardent prayer. Encourage family members to express their joys, worries, and requests for prayers via open dialogue. Gather often as a family to pray, asking God to lead, protect, and bless you. Instill a culture of prayer in your family so that it becomes a normal part of everyday life.

Self-Reflection Questions

How can you better comprehend the unique obstacles and difficulties that each family member has so that you can pray more effectively for their needs?

_____

_____

_____

_____

_____

_____

_____

_____

_____

_____

_____

_____

What recent indications of conflict or division have you seen in your family? How can you strategically pray to counteract these unfavorable forces and try to reestablish peace and unity?

_____

_____

_____

_____

_____

_____

_____

_____

_____

_____

_____

_____

_____

Which Bible scriptures or chapters strike you as being sources of blessing, safety, and direction for your family? How are they to be included in your prayers?

_____

_____

_____

_____

_____

_____

_____

_____

_____

_____

_____

_____

_____

_____

What concrete steps can you take to improve your marriage or the marriages in your family? What can you do in prayer to make God's mercy and wisdom visible in these relationships?

_____

_____

_____

_____

_____

_____

_____

_____

_____

_____

_____

_____

_____

What actions can you take to foster positive parent-child relationships and foster a climate of support, love, and open dialogue within your family? How may prayer be a key component in developing these bonds?

_____

Think about the way you pray as a family now and the place of religion in your household. How can you foster a culture of prayer in your family where asking God for help, protection, and blessings becomes a normal part of everyday life?

_____

_____

_____

Life-Transforming Exercises

1. Personal prayer journals: Assign one prayer book to each family member. Encourage them to record their own prayer requests, issues, and aspirations in writing. Include your family's particular needs from their diaries in your prayers when you do so, and encourage them to do the same for one another.

2. Scripture Declarations: Pick texts from the Bible that speak to your family's needs and difficulties. Put them in plain sight throughout the home by writing them on index cards or sticky notes. Family members should be urged to read these passages every day, reflect on them, and use them as the basis for their declarations and prayers.

3. Family Prayer Time: Choose a regular time for your family to pray. Gather as a family, whether it is for dinner, just before bed, or once a week at a set time. Encourage each family member to express their

happiness, worries, and requests for prayers at this time. Lead the prayer and offer up prayers for one another alternately.

4. Prayer Walks: Use this time to pray over the home you share with your family. Make prayer rounds of your house, each room, and the neighborhood. Pray especially for the needs, safety, and spiritual development of each member of your family while you walk. Request that God bless your house and envelop it in His presence.

5. Service: Through deliberate acts of service, show your family that you love and care about them. Make note of their requirements and look into doable approaches to assist and elevate them. Let your actions reflect your prayers for their well-being and growth, whether it's through assisting with domestic duties, lending a sympathetic ear, or pleasantly surprising them with tiny acts of kindness.

Strategy 5: Your Past: Ending the Reign of Guilt, Shame, and Regret

Key Lessons

1. Embrace God's Forgiveness: This tactic teaches us to recognize and embrace God's forgiveness for our prior transgressions. Shirer highlights that through prayer, we may truly accept God's forgiveness and experience genuine freedom since God's love and grace are stronger than whatever guilt, shame, or regret we may be carrying.

2. Let Go of Shame: Shirer emphasizes the damaging nature of shame and how it may prevent us from experiencing life to the fullest. We may let go of the weight and enable God's healing and restoration to occur by confessing our previous mistakes and feelings of shame to Him in prayer. This will help us to go ahead with confidence and a refreshed sense of self-worth.

3. Replace regret with redemption: This lesson places a strong emphasis on the redemptive power of God. Shirer advises us to give our regrets to God and put our faith in His capacity to use them for good and redeem us rather than wallowing in regret and letting it define us. We may convert our regrets into chances for development and change by asking God to utilize our experiences for His benefit.

4. Challenge Negative Self-Talk: Shirer helps readers identify and combat the self-defeating thoughts that often come from their history. We may replace self-criticism with God's truth and confirmations of our identity in Christ by strategically praying. To break away from the grasp of a negative self-perception, this lesson instructs us to match our thoughts with God's Word and speak life-giving words over ourselves.

5. Live in the Present: The last lesson exhorts us to let go of the past and put all of our attention on living completely in the present. To truly enjoy the rich life God intends for us, Shirer highlights the significance of letting go of the regrets, errors, and humiliation from the past. By strategically praying, we may give God control over our history, enabling Him to heal our wounds and give us the ability to live in the present with meaning, joy, and freedom.

Self-Reflection Questions

Have you accepted God's forgiveness for your previous transgressions fully? How can you better comprehend and embrace His unending grace?

_____

_____

_____

_____

_____

_____

_____

_____

_____

_____

_____

_____

_____

Consider the areas of your life where guilt has prevented you from progressing. How can you pray to God about those things and enable Him to heal and restore you so that you may be free?

_____

_____

_____

_____

_____

_____

_____

What old regrets do you still harbor? How can you give them to God and believe that He would use them for good and bring about your redemption?

_____

_____

_____

_____

_____

_____

_____

How often do you indulge in self-deprecation or negative self-talk? How can you counteract such unfavorable ideas with God's truth and reminders of your identity in Christ?

_____

_____

_____

_____

_____

_____

_____

_____

_____

_____

_____

_____

_____

Do you primarily focus on the here and now or do you regularly find yourself obsessing on errors, regrets, or humiliation from the past? How can you let go of the past and accept the bountiful life God has prepared for you right now?

_____

_____

_____

_____

_____

_____

_____

_____

_____

_____

_____

_____

How can you integrate prayer strategically into your
life, with an emphasis on letting go of the past and

embracing forgiveness, redemption, and self-acceptance? How can you make prayer a regular habit on your path to recovery and liberation?

_____

_____

_____

_____

_____

_____

_____

_____

_____

_____

_____

_____

Life-Transforming Exercises

1. "Letter of Release": Compose a sincere letter to God in which you convey all your regrets, remorse, and humiliation. Without holding back, express all of your sentiments. Then, as a symbolic act of giving those burdens to God, tear up or burn the letter as a sign of submission. Make a surrendered prayer while you do this, asking God to take charge of your past and provide healing and restoration.

2. "Scriptural Affirmations": List the important scriptures in the Bible that describe God's mercy, grace, and forgiveness. Put these scriptures on index cards or sticky notes and post them where you will see them often, such as on your refrigerator, bathroom mirror, or desk. Every time you come across one of these affirmations, speak it out loud and allow the truth of God's Word to replace your negative self-talk and serve as a constant reminder of your identity in Christ.

3. "Renaming Your Past": Spend some time in prayer asking God to show you how He sees your history. Ask

Him to provide His perspective on your life and experiences, and then be willing to listen. As you acquire understanding, think about giving your history new names that are consistent with God's truth and redemption. If you were ashamed of a failed relationship, for instance, reframe it as a time of learning and development that helped you prepare for a brighter future.

4. "Gratitude Journal": Begin a gratitude journal to concentrate on the advantages and lessons you've learned from your prior experiences. Write down the wonderful experiences that have helped to mold you, and be grateful for God's constant presence in your life. Recognizing the positive aspects of your history might alter your viewpoint and promote feelings of appreciation and joy.

5. "Prayer Walk of Release": Go on a prayer walk in a serene outdoor setting to let go of the burden of guilt, shame, and regret. Pray aloud as you walk, giving God your whole heart and your concerns. Make physical motions along the way, such as raising your hands and lifting them to the sky, that suggest you are letting go of those responsibilities. Prayer of appreciation for God's healing and freedom in your life should be spoken at the end of the walk.

Strategy 6: Your Fears: Confronting Your Worries, Claiming Your Calling

Key Lessons

1. Recognizing the Source of Fear Shirer stresses the need of understanding the origin of our worries. We may decide the proper course of action by determining if our anxieties are a result of God's conviction or the enemy's deceit. Through prayer, we may better understand the truth and face our fears by using God's Word as our compass.

2. Scripture-based prayer: Shirer exhorts women to use Scripture as a potent tool to battle their worries. We may bring our thoughts into agreement with God's truth and lay hold of His promises by looking for pertinent passages and integrating them into our prayers. Scripture-based prayer builds our faith and gives us a firm platform on which to confront our worries.

3. Destroying Fear's Strongholds: Shirer highlights the need of locating and eliminating the strongholds that fear

has over our life. These strongholds might take the form of harmful thought habits, illogical beliefs, or behavior patterns that keep us mired in anxiety. These strongholds may be targeted and destroyed via deliberate prayer, and their place can be taken by God's truth and freedom.

4. Giving Control to God: Shirer emphasizes the need of giving control to God while facing our worries. She exhorts women to have faith in God's omnipotence, discernment, and well-thought-out plans. We may find calm by giving Him our worries and concerns because we know He is in charge and will help us through any circumstance.

5. Accepting our Calling: Shirer encourages women to face their concerns and openly accept the calling that God has given them. She serves as a reminder that our inability to fully embrace and use our special abilities is often caused by fear. We may conquer our anxieties, unlock our potential, and boldly follow the purpose that God has given us through ardent prayer.

Self-Reflection Questions

What particular phobias or concerns have you noticed in your life? How do these apprehensions square with God's promises and truth as revealed in the Bible?

_____

_____

_____

_____

_____

_____

_____

_____

_____

_____

_____

_____

How do you now overcome your worries with prayer and Scripture? Do you have any particular verses or paragraphs that speak to you and may serve as the basis for your prayers?

_____

_____

_____

_____

_____

_____

_____

_____

_____

_____

_____

_____

_____

Think about any strongholds that fear may have built in your life for a bit. What harmful habits of thinking or actions have you profoundly ingrained? How can you strategically pray to overthrow these fortresses and establish God's truth in their place?

_____

_____

_____

_____

_____

_____

_____

_____

_____

_____

_____

_____

_____

What aspects of your life do you find difficult to give God full authority over? How can you put more faith in His omnipotence and wisdom, knowing that He is with you at all times and leading your steps?

_____

_____

_____

_____

_____

_____

_____

_____

_____

_____

_____

_____

_____

Think about your God-given purpose as well as any aspirations or abilities you may have suppressed out of fear. How have your anxieties prevented you from accepting and living out your mission fully? Ask God in prayer for the courage and strength to go forth with confidence in His guidance and provision.

_____

_____

_____

_____

_____

_____

_____

_____

_____

_____

_____

How do you develop a regular, deliberate prayer practice that gives voice to your anxieties and fears? What doable actions can you do to strengthen your prayer practice and make it a powerful, transforming tool for facing and conquering fear?

_____

_____

_____

_____

_____

_____

_____

_____

_____

_____

_____

_____

Life-Transforming Exercises

1. Fear Inventory: Take some time to consider and list the particular concerns and anxieties that are now preventing you from moving forward or giving you worry. Identify your anxieties honestly and completely, realizing how they affect your thoughts, feelings, and behavior.

2. Scriptural Declarations: Choose three texts that express God's promises of bravery, power, and serenity about fear. Create digital reminders on your phone or write them out on index cards. Repeat these verses aloud to yourself as you go about your day to help you remember God's truth and control over your anxieties.

3. Demolition of a Stronghold: Pick one particularly powerful fear that you desire to destroy and replace with

God's truth. Declare your determination to face and destroy this stronghold with God's assistance in a letter or prayer addressed to it. Give particular examples of the unfavorable attitudes or conduct that are connected to this fear and enlist God's help and power to supplant them with His truth.

4. Surrender and Release: Find some quiet time and a place where you may give your anxieties and fears to God. Release each fear into God's loving and skilled hands in your imagination. As you let go, offer a prayer of submission in which you declare your faith in God's purpose and His capacity to see you through any difficulty.

5. Step Into Your Calling: Consider the goals and aspirations you have put on hold out of fear. Choose a single action or step you can do right now to get closer to your calling. It might be as simple as looking into possibilities or as daring as enrolling in a course or getting in touch with a mentor. Put this step in writing and resolve to execute it, believing that God will lead you as you work toward your goal.

Strategy 7: Your Purity: Staying Strong in Your Most Susceptible Places

Key Lessons

1. Recognize your weak spots: The first step in maintaining your virginity is to identify the places on your body where you are most prone to temptation. A tailored prayer plan may be created to help you overcome your weaknesses by taking an honest inventory of them, whether they be situations, people, or triggers.

2. Protect your mind: Decisions and behaviors are often influenced by our ideas. Shirer stresses the need to actively protect your mind from impurities and harmful influences. You may fortify your mind and safeguard your purity by immersing yourself in God's Word, reflecting on His truth, and swapping out unclean ideas with good and pure ones.

3. Demand accountability: Finding a group that is supportive of you is essential in the fight for purity. Relationships with dependable people who support your dedication to purity might provide you with the support

and responsibility you need to persevere. Ask God in prayer to guide you to other Christians who share your beliefs so they may go with you.

4. Use prayer as a weapon: Prayer is an effective means of sustaining chastity. Shirer emphasizes the value of fervently and specifically praying to God about your difficulties, temptations, and weaknesses. You may experience miraculous breakthroughs and develop the fortitude to withstand temptation by giving your aspirations to God and asking for His help and direction.

5. Celebrate advancement and engage in self-compassion: It's important to acknowledge and rejoice in even the tiniest achievements on the road to purity. Shirer advises adopting a mentality of self-compassion rather than concentrating on errors or failures in the past. Keep in mind that progress is a process and setbacks are temporary. You may find the courage to continue on your path to purity by giving yourself grace, recognizing your progress, and relying on God's unfailing love.

Self-Reflection Questions

Have you given any thought to where you are most susceptible to losing your purity? How can you create a prayer plan to combat the situations, people, or triggers that might cause you to wander from God?

_____

_____

_____

_____

_____

_____

_____

_____

_____

_____

_____

_____

How consciously do you protect your mind against
tainted and harmful influences? Are you consistently
spending time in God's Word and reframing your
doubts with His truth? What actions may you do to
bolster your intellect and safeguard your purity?

_____

_____

_____

_____

_____

_____

_____

_____

_____

_____

_____

_____

_____

Do you belong to a godly group of Christians who encourage and hold each other accountable in your quest for holiness? If not, how can you find people who support you and build connections that will keep you going strong?

_____

_____

_____

_____

_____

_____

_____

_____

_____

_____

_____

_____

_____

How often do you use prayer as a tool in the struggle for chastity? Are you praying fervently and specifically to God about your difficulties, temptations, and weaknesses? How can you strengthen your prayer life and ask for His support and direction in this regard?

_____

_____

_____

_____

_____

_____

_____

_____

_____

_____

_____

_____

_____

Are you rejoicing in your efforts to keep purity, no matter how little? Or do you often dwell on your previous failings and errors? How can you manage this road with an attitude of self-compassion and grace for yourself?

_____

_____

_____

_____

_____

_____

_____

_____

_____

_____

What actions have you made that have resulted in favorable outcomes when you think back on your path to purity? What still needs development and improvement? How can you continue to advance in your quest for purity by leaning on God's unfailing love and relying on His strength?

Life-Transforming Exercises

1. Susceptibility Inventory: Take an inventory of your vulnerabilities when it comes to preserving the purity and note them. Noting certain situations, connections, or triggers that can send you astray, jot them down in a diary or notebook.

2. Purity Affirmations: Create a list of uplifting and inspiring purity-related affirmations. Put them in plain sight in places like your office, bedroom mirror, and dashboard of your automobile by writing them on index cards or sticky notes. Every day, state these affirmations publicly and with conviction. Let these affirmations act as potent reminders of your dedication to purity and of your Christ-centered identity.

3. Accountability Partner: Look for a reliable accountability partner who values chastity. meet often to talk about struggles, triumphs, and prayer needs. Create a system of check-ins and support one another as you pursue purity.

4. Prayer Strategy Plan: To address the areas of vulnerability you identified, develop a particular prayer strategy plan. Create specific prayers that include scripture and your requests and address each vulnerable

area. Make time each day set aside to pray sincerely and explicitly for chastity in those areas.

5. Keep a thankfulness and progress notebook to acknowledge your accomplishments in maintaining purity, no matter how modest they may be. List at least one aspect of your trip for which you are thankful each day. Keep track of your advancements and development, marking the times when God has given you courage and direction.

Strategy 8: Your Pressures: Reclaiming Peace, Rest, and Contentment

Key Lessons

1. Recognize the cause of your difficulties: Recognizing the stressors in your life and eliminating them is the first step in regaining calm, relaxation, and satisfaction. Women are urged by Priscilla Shirer to evaluate their sources of stress and worry openly. Knowing the underlying problems can help you address them in prayer and seek God's direction for lasting peace.

2. Prioritize rest and self-care: Despite life's responsibilities, Shirer stresses the need of prioritizing rest and self-care. She tells the audience that caring for oneself is not self-indulgent but rather necessary for general well-being. You may refuel your soul and confront difficulties with fresh power and clarity by establishing limits, engaging in self-compassion, and scheduling rest periods into your daily schedule.

3. Fight the enemy's lies: The devil often utilizes stress and worry to draw our attention away from God's truth and rob us of our serenity. Shirer exhorts women to

recognize the misconceptions and destructive thinking patterns that fuel their fears. She shows how to swap out those falsehoods with God's promises and affirmations of truth, restoring peace and satisfaction in the process. She does this via strategic prayer and the authority of God's Word.

4. Give up control and trust God: This tactic emphasizes the value of giving up control and believing in God's omnipotence. Readers are not required to bear the weight of the whole world on their shoulders, as Shirer reminds them. She helps women give their problems, fears, and stresses to God via prayer, knowing that He is in charge and cares about them. A greater feeling of tranquility and happiness is possible when control is given up.

5. Adopt a grateful mindset: Gratitude can change our viewpoint and provide satisfaction despite challenges. Shirer exhorts women to consciously dwell on God's faithfulness and the benefits in their life to develop a mentality of appreciation. Women may enjoy more peace, pleasure, and happiness by deciding to express gratitude, especially in trying situations, as they acknowledge God's kindness and provision.

Self-Reflection Questions

Have you taken the effort to pinpoint the exact pressure points and causes of stress in your life? Are you prepared to pray to God about these difficulties?

_____

_____

_____

_____

_____

_____

_____

_____

_____

_____

_____

_____

_____

_____

How can you prioritize rest and self-care in your daily schedule? What can you do to make sure you have time for yourself despite the demands of life?

_____

_____

_____

_____

_____

_____

_____

_____

_____

_____

_____

_____

_____

Do you have any ingrained negative thinking patterns or self-defeating falsehoods that exacerbate your worries? How can you use scripture and prayer to confront these falsehoods with God's truth?

_____

_____

_____

_____

_____

_____

_____

_____

_____

_____

_____

_____

_____

Where in your life do you find it challenging to relinquish control and believe in God's omnipotence? How can you strengthen your dependence on Him and your trust in those areas?

_____

_____

_____

_____

_____

_____

_____

_____

_____

_____

_____

_____

_____

_____

How can you consciously practice being grateful even
when faced with difficulties and demands? How can
you remind yourself of God's goodness and benefits
in your life? What habits can you develop?

_____

_____

_____

_____

_____

_____

_____

_____

_____

_____

_____

_____

Are there any particular stresses or anxieties you
need to confide in God about in prayer, knowing that
He will take care of them for you? What actions can

you do to let go of these responsibilities and have more peace and satisfaction in your day-to-day life?

_____

_____

_____

_____

_____

_____

_____

_____

_____

_____

Life-Transforming Exercises

1. Pressure Inventory: Take a moment to think about the numerous strains and tensions in your life. Make a list or keep a notebook where you may detail the precise pressure sources. You will become more aware of the issues you should cover in your prayers as a result of this practice.

2. Create a Restful Routine: Create a restful routine with a focus on rejuvenation and self-care. Choose peaceful pursuits and plan them into your daily or weekly calendar. It may be reading, going for a stroll in the woods, being attentive, or doing anything you want to do. Commit to scheduling these things consistently.

3. thinking Transformation: Start keeping track of your thoughts to see if any persistently unfavorable thinking patterns fuel your anxiety. Once you've discovered these tendencies, confront them with the truth of God. Choose verses from the Bible that directly refute the falsehoods you often think about yourself or your situation. When

those bad ideas come, write them down and say them out.

4. Create a "Surrender Box" where you may tangibly give God your worries, tensions, and concerns. As a sign of resignation, write them down on pieces of paper and put them in the box. Go to the box whenever you are feeling overburdened, pray over its contents, and intentionally give them to God.

5. Gratitude Journaling: Begin a gratitude diary in which you may list three items every day for which you are thankful. Spend a few minutes every morning and evening thanking God for all the blessings in your life. Possessing the practice of thankfulness may alter your viewpoint and bring you feelings of serenity and satisfaction.

Strategy 9: Your Hurts: Turning Bitterness to Forgiveness

Key Lessons

1. Carrying unresolved sorrows and anger in our hearts has negative impacts on our spiritual development, as Priscilla Shirer emphasizes. She makes a point of saying that these scars might impede our connection with God and keep us from experiencing His pleasure and serenity. To begin the process of healing and regeneration, we must first acknowledge the effect of our wounds.

2. Forgiveness is a formidable tool in our fight against the devil. Shirer describes forgiveness as a powerful act of spiritual warfare. We deny the adversary a stronghold in our lives by choosing to forgive those who have wronged us. By releasing us from the bonds of resentment, forgiveness allows God to heal and restore us.

3. Forgiveness is a path that often requires time and work; it is not a one-time occurrence, according to Shirer. She exhorts readers to keep trying to ask for forgiveness even if it could mean going back over

upsetting times and feelings. We may find genuine healing and freedom from the shackles of bitterness by giving our wounds to God and letting Him work in our hearts.

4. God's limitless forgiveness toward us is something Shirer reminds us of, and it helps us grant forgiveness. Thinking about how kind and merciful God is inspiring us to forgive others in the same way. We may resist the need to cling to resentment and instead choose to provide love and compassion to those who have hurt us by accepting the reality of our forgiveness.

5. Prayer is the key to forgiveness: This chapter highlights the importance of prayer in the forgiving process. Shirer exhorts readers to pray to God about their problems and troubles, asking Him to help them and give them the ability to forgive. By praying purposefully and strategically, we ask God to work in our hearts so that we may let go of the weight of unforgiveness and enjoy the freedom and peace that come with it.

Self-Reflection Questions

Have you identified any unresolved grievances or resentment in your heart that could be impeding your spiritual development and connection to God?

_____

_____

_____

How can you use forgiveness as a potent weapon in your spiritual battle? Do you need to forgive anybody or something in particular, to be released from the grip of the enemy?

_____

_____

_____

_____

_____

_____

_____

_____

_____

_____

_____

_____

Consider a moment when you went through the process of forgiving someone. How did you proceed, and what did you discover along the way?

_____

_____

_____

_____

_____

_____

_____

_____

_____

_____

_____

_____

_____

**What effect does remembering God's forgiveness of
you have on your capacity to forgive others? Do you
encounter any obstacles or difficulties in forgiving
someone fully?**

_____

_____

_____

_____

_____

_____

_____

_____

_____

_____

_____

_____

_____

_____

In what ways in your life might prayer be a doorway to forgiveness? How can you consciously include prayer in your quest for recovery and resentment release?

_____

_____

_____

_____

_____

_____

_____

_____

_____

_____

_____

_____

_____

Think about how your heart and connections are doing right now. Do you have any particular grievances or incidents of resentment that you need to pray to God about? How do you enlist His aid in navigating the process of forgiving in certain circumstances?

_____

_____

_____

_____

_____

_____

_____

_____

_____

_____

_____

_____

Life-Transforming Exercises

1. Reflective journaling: Schedule time specifically for thinking about your wounds and places of resentment. Write about your experiences in a notebook, expressing your anguish, and naming the people or circumstances that contributed to it. Investigate your feelings, ideas, and any patterns or themes that keep coming up. You will obtain clarity and understanding of the places that call for forgiveness as a result of this practice.

2. Prayer of Release: Say a targeted and purposeful prayer of release in which you give God your wounds and resentment. Find a peaceful area and give Him your heart. You should express your hurt, rage, and resentment while letting go of your need for vengeance and justice. Ask God to replace these burdens with His peace and healing instead.

3. Identify Triggers and Responses: Give some thought to the situations or people who make you feel resentful or bitter. It may be specific phrases, circumstances, or

conversations. Make a plan of action after you have identified these triggers. Create deliberate responses to help you deal with these triggers with grace and forgiveness, such as taking deep breaths, repeating a selected Bible passage, or taking a break to pray.

4. Exercise empathy and compassion by picking someone who has wounded you, and making an effort to see things from their point of view. Consider what could have motivated them to behave as they did by putting yourself in their position. By cultivating empathy and compassion, this activity helps pave the way for reconciliation and recovery.

5. Compose a Letter of Forgiveness: Compose a sincere letter of apology to the person who caused you harm. Write out your feelings, describing your pain as well as your choice to forgive them. Be clear about the deeds or words that hurt you, and intentionally let go of the resentment attached to those memories. You have the option of sending the letter or keeping it for further contemplation.

Strategy 10: Your Relationships: Uniting in a Common Cause Amen

Key Lessons

1. The Strength of United Prayer: Shirer emphasizes the tremendous power that comes from cooperating in prayer with other Christians. She stresses the need of building unified connections and engaging in meaningful prayer collaborations. Women may experience a collective force that vanquishes spiritual foes and brings about change via unified prayer.

2. Identifying and Praying for connections: In this chapter, Shirer exhorts readers to recognize important connections in their life and resolve to dedicate themselves to praying particularly for each one. She underlines how important it is to pray for these partnerships' harmony, healing, and spiritual development. Women may observe the healing and restoration that result from the power of prayer by consciously praying for loved ones.

3. Guarding Against Division: Shirer discusses the enemy's efforts for sowing discord in interpersonal relationships and stresses the need of identifying and thwarting these tactics via prayer. She exhorts readers to

pray for discernment and wisdom to deal with disagreements and disputes lovingly and graciously. Women may protect their relationships against the enemy's efforts to divide and conquer by fervently praying for harmony and reconciliation.

4. Strengthening Marriages and Family Bonds: Shirer emphasizes the need of giving prayer special attention to strengthening marriages and family ties. She offers doable methods for praying for partners, kids, and other family members. Women may build an environment of love, peace, and spiritual development within their families by praying deliberately and specifically, which can strengthen relationships over time.

5. Extending Prayer Beyond Personal Circles: In this chapter, Shirer exhorts women to extend their prayers beyond their close friends and family and to offer up their intercession for larger groups of people and concerns. She stresses the significance of prayer for the universal church, local congregations, and missionaries across the world. Women may have a tremendous effect and take part in a greater movement of change and revival by joining together in prayer for the expansion of God's kingdom.

Self-Reflection Questions

How have you personally experienced the effectiveness of unified prayer? Think of a time when group prayer resulted in a great breakthrough or prayer being answered.

_____

_____

_____

_____

_____

_____

_____

_____

_____

_____

_____

_____

_____

Think for a minute about the important relationships in your life that may benefit from focused, purposeful prayer. How can you promise to pray for these relationships' development, healing, and unification?

_____

_____

_____

_____

_____

_____

_____

_____

_____

_____

_____

_____

_____

Have you seen any dividing strategies in your relationships? How can you pray about these issues and ask God for help in handling disagreements graciously and lovingly?

_____

_____

_____

_____

_____

_____

_____

_____

_____

_____

_____

_____

_____

_____

Think about how your marriage and family are doing. How can you pray deliberately and specifically to build and prioritize these ties? What particular aspects of your family's life need mending or development?

_____

_____

_____

_____

_____

_____

_____

_____

_____

_____

_____

_____

_____

How can you pray for larger groups and concerns instead of just your own family and friends? Consider how you may fervently pray for the church, regional congregations, and international relief efforts.

Think about how you can promote harmony and change in the people you interact with and the larger community. What measures can you take to pray fervently and strategically such that it affects others around you? How can you use prayer to deliberately pursue God's kingdom and His purposes?

_____

_____

_____

_____

<u>Life-Transforming Exercises</u>

1. Establish a prayer partnership diary in which you and a close friend or accountability partner may record specific prayer requests for one another's relationships. Establish regular periods for praying together and keeping a prayer journal. Celebrate the times of unity and victories you see in each other's life.

2. Make a list of the important connections in your life that may benefit from concentrated prayer. Take some time to make this list. List the names of any relatives, friends, coworkers, or any people you feel moved to pray for. Write down any particular prayer requests or areas where you feel there is a need for healing, restoration, or development next to each person's name. Use this list as a regular reference throughout your prayer periods.

3. Practice reconciliation and forgiveness: Consider any tense or strained relationships in your life. Consider moving toward forgiveness and reconciliation in a spirit of prayer. To address the parties concerned and ask for His assistance in mending any wounds or misunderstandings, seek God's counsel. Commit to prayer as part of your implementation practice for God's mercy and discernment as you handle these difficult talks.

4. A prayer map or chart representing your neighborhood's church and community should be made. Determine the particular church ministries or places that need prayer, as well as the difficulties or problems in the neighborhood that call for God's involvement. Commit to prayer often for these issues, asking God for his insight and direction in altering people's lives and circumstances.

5. Global Missions Prayer Calendar: Create a prayer calendar that emphasizes global missions and the work that missionaries throughout the globe are doing. Pray daily for a certain nation or area, as well as the needs and difficulties experienced by the missionaries working there. Allow God to direct you in terms of how you may also assist and give to these missions practically. Keep your heart open to His guidance.

Self Evaluation Exercises

How has reading "Fervent" changed the way you pray? Think about the particular ways the book has affected the way you pray and interact with God.

_____

_____

_____

_____

_____

_____

_____

_____

_____

_____

_____

_____

Have the techniques in the book helped you identify any particular weak points or struggles in your life? If yes, explain how you intend to use targeted, strategic prayer to meet these problems.

_____

_____

_____

_____

_____

_____

_____

_____

_____

_____

_____

_____

_____

How have you adopted the idea of ardent prayer alliances and collective prayer with others? Have you made an effort to build deliberate prayer communities? How have they influenced your prayer life?

_____

_____

_____

_____

_____

_____

_____

_____

_____

_____

_____

_____

_____

How have you used the ideas of strategic prayer in your interpersonal interactions? Give an example of a time when prayer was used strategically to settle a dispute or promote harmony in your relationships.

_____

_____

_____

_____

_____

_____

_____

_____

_____

_____

_____

_____

_____

After reading the book, have you made any particular plans for improving your prayer life? Think back on your progress toward reaching these objectives and any future modifications you may need to make.

Think about the section on praying for strong family and marital ties. Have you made a conscious effort to pray for your spouse and your family? Describe any favorable modifications to your family's dynamics that you have seen as a consequence of these prayers.

_____

_____

_____

_____

_____

_____

_____

_____

_____

_____

_____

_____

_____

Have you included the local community, churches in your area, and international missions in your prayers? Describe how your perspective and feeling of purpose have changed as a result of praying for the expansion of God's kingdom.

_____

_____

_____

_____

_____

_____

_____

_____

_____

_____

_____

_____

_____

After reading about the effectiveness of scripture-based prayer, how have you included scripture in your prayer life? Give an example of a scripture or paragraph that has grown to mean a lot to you throughout your prayer journey.

_____

_____

_____

_____

_____

_____

_____

_____

_____

_____

_____

_____

_____

_____

Consider any difficulties or problems you encountered while putting the techniques in the book into practice. What actions can you do to get beyond these obstacles and keep developing your prayer life?

_____

_____

_____

_____

_____

_____

_____

_____

_____

_____

_____

_____

_____

What significant realizations or lessons have you drawn from "Fervent" as the workbook's conclusion draws near? How do you intend to use these teachings in your everyday life and continue to develop as a prayer?

Made in the USA
Coppell, TX
09 October 2023